LIGHT AT GROUND ZERO:
ST. PAUL'S CHAPEL AFTER 9/11

krystyna sanderson

Square Halo Books

First Edition 2003
Copyright ©2003 Square Halo Books
P.O. Box 18954, Baltimore, MD 21206
www.SquareHaloBooks.com

In Christian art, the square halo identified a living person presumed to be a saint. Square Halo Books is devoted to publishing works that present contextually sensitive biblical studies, and practical instruction consistent with the Doctrines of the Reformation. The goal of Square Halo Books is to provide materials useful for encouraging and equipping the saints.

ISBN 0-9658798-4-4
Library of Congress Control Number: 2003105193

Printed in Korea

LIGHT AT GROUND ZERO:
ST. PAUL'S CHAPEL AFTER 9/11

Krystyna Sanderson

Square Halo Books

First Edition 2003
Copyright ©2003 Square Halo Books
P.O. Box 18954, Baltimore, MD 21206
www.SquareHaloBooks.com

In Christian art, the square halo identified a living person presumed to be a saint. Square Halo Books is devoted to publishing works that present contextually sensitive biblical studies, and practical instruction consistent with the Doctrines of the Reformation. The goal of Square Halo Books is to provide materials useful for encouraging and equipping the saints.

ISBN 0-9658798-4-4
Library of Congress Control Number: 2003105193

Printed in Korea

FOREWORD

on september 12, after having escaped the maelstrom of 9/11, I returned to Lower Manhattan to survey the damage to saint paul's chapel—just yards away from

where Building 5 of the World Trade Center stood—and to find ways to be helpful in the rescue effort. At that point we assumed there would be many survivors. My heart was pounding as I walked down Broadway from my apartment in Greenwich Village, not knowing what I might find. I assumed the chapel had been demolished. When I saw the spire still standing, I was overwhelmed. It took my breath away. Opening the door to enter St. Paul's was an extraordinary experience. Except for a layer of ash and soot, the building survived unscathed. Many proclaimed that "St. Paul's had been spared." It seemed clear to me that if this was true, it was not because we were holier than anyone who died across the street; it was because we now had a big job to do.

Taking this challenge to heart, we set up a cold drink concession and hot food service four days later for the rescue workers, and men from our shelter, among others, proudly flipped burgers at what came to be called affectionately "the Barbecue on Broadway." The relief ministry at St. Paul's was supported by the labor of three local institutions—the Seamen's Church Institute, General Theological Seminary, and St. Paul's in the parish of Trinity Church—and by volunteers from all over the country. More than 5,000 people used their special gifts to transform Saint Paul's Chapel into a place of rest and refuge. Musicians, clergy, podiatrists, lawyers, soccer moms, and folks of every imaginable type poured coffee, swept floors, took out the trash, and served more than half a million meals. Emerging at St. Paul's was a dynamic I think of as a "reciprocity of gratitude"—a circle of thanksgiving—in which volunteers and rescue and recovery workers tried to outdo each other with acts of kindness and love, leaving both giver and receiver changed. This circle of gratitude was infectious, and I hope it continues to spread.

T. S. Eliot's poem "Little Gidding" opens with the words, "Midwinter spring is its own season." The period from the terrorist attacks to the end of the recovery efforts at Ground Zero was its own season, lasting 260 days. Although the calendar tells us that it lasted for three seasons—fall, winter, and spring—many of us have little recollection of any climate changes. We just got up, day after day, dressed accordingly, and went about the monumental task of trying to make sense out of insanity, bring order out of chaos, and reclaim humanity from the violence that sought to make human life less human. This was also a season of remembrance as we mourned the loss of loved ones. It was a season of improvisation as we tried, often at our wit's end, to respond to the needs emerging from these never before experienced acts of terrorism. It was a season of renewal as we sought to look toward a day when our commonalities will overcome our

divisions, when compassion will overcome violence, and kindness will swallow up hatred. Ultimately, what began in hatred evolved into, in the words from that great song from the musical *Rent,* a "season of love." It was a season in which people of love and goodwill, compassion and generosity, sought to practice the art of radical hospitality.

Capturing this remarkable experience in photographs, Krystyna Sanderson worked tirelessly day in and day out. She offered her own labor of love. I am grateful to Krystyna for her dedication and hard work. Future generations will also be grateful for this glimpse into a unique chapter in the history of our city and our country.

The chapel that once housed massage therapists, tired workers, compassionate volunteers and thousands of love notes carefully colored by schoolchildren and displayed upon its walls has now been restored to its pre-9/11 grandeur. The relief ministry at St. Paul's came to its necessary end. But the images in this album enable us to revisit Saint Paul's Chapel during that pivotal time, and in some small way, keep alive the spirit of love and goodwill that bathed all who entered its doors during the ministry of hospitality offered to the heroes and heroines who gave so much of themselves working at Ground Zero.

The Rev. Lyndon Harris,
Associate for Ministries at St. Paul's Chapel

was enveloped in a subdued light, a murmur of hushed voices, a sacred spirit, undeniable, almost tactile. The interior of the chapel with its pastel pinks and blues and its delicate Waterford crystal chandeliers could offer no greater contrast to the monochromatic moonlike landscape of Ground Zero with its associations of dread, horror and agony. St. Paul's was a welcoming fireplace where all who entered could warm themselves from the elements and from the cold spectacle outside.

For seven months my camera and I were witnesses, and I hope also instruments, of God's radical grace, mercy and love at St. Paul's. During this time I created over 2,500 images. My ministry was to witness and to record the work of the Holy Spirit in action. I loved the brilliant morning light pouring through the east window over the altar, and the warm late afternoon light from the south windows bathing the chapel in gold. The 18-century symmetry of the chapel formed an ideal backdrop for the rainbow colors of children's cards and letters and the large and small banners from all over the world. Here God's love was poured out through thousands of hearts stretched to the breaking point, through sore hands and aching feet. Workers and volunteers shared their lives, their stories, a cup of soup or coffee. We prayed and cried, sometimes alone, sometimes together. We hugged, and we refrained from hugging.

The ashes of those who perished were everywhere—on the boots of the relief workers, on our clothes, in the air we breathed. We all knew we were walking on holy ground. Like diamonds that are created when carbon is under tremendous pressure, diamonds of heroism and love emerged from the explosion of 9/11. I witnessed these diamonds emitting a luminosity too bright to capture on film, a light that lightens the darkness of disbelief, shock, incomprehension, and grief, the light of God's love and mercy and grace.

Krystyna Sanderson

thank Trinity Church for allowing me to photograph this historic event at St. Paul's Chapel. The Rev. Lyndon Harris invited me to photograph St. Paul's and was the guiding spirit of the relief effort throughout its whole existence of almost nine months. His enthusiastic support and loving care upheld not only me but all who passed through the doors of St. Paul's during that time. Five other guardian angels, Katherine Avery, Sister Grace of the Sisters of St. Margaret, Courtney V. Cowart, Martin Cowart, and the Rev. Dr. Frederic B. Burnham were ever-present beacons of welcome. The Nine Twelve Community, formed to carry on the vision born from the months of relief work, offered help and encouragement.

Saint Paul's Episcopal Church in Edenton, North Carolina, and especially its rector, the Rev. Thomas M. Rickenbaker, strongly supported the ministry at St. Paul's the whole way through. Generous grants from Robert Sanderson, Mary Parker, Bob and Ellen Groff and Claudia Breese and the Visual Arts Committee and Worship Commission of First Presbyterian Church, Portland, Oregon provided needed financial support. My husband, Colin, contributed countless hours of editing and his continuing emotional and spiritual support. James Romaine, Jenny Neat, Jennifer Schmidt, and everyone at Square Halo Books have contributed untold prayer, expertise and labor in making this book a reality.

I am grateful to many in my Episcopal Church community. Bishop George E. Packard and Andrew J. N. Gary have been heartening advocates. The Episcopal Church and Visual Arts (ECVA) has encouraged my art in the life of the Episcopal Church. I am especially grateful to Bishop Frank T. Griswold, Presiding Bishop of the Episcopal Church, and his wife Phoebe for their support of ECVA. My thanks to *Episcopal Life,* especially its editor Jerry Hames, and to Episcopal Relief and Development for their patronage. My home parish of Grace Church in New York has been a constant source of support and inspiration, especially the Rev. Anne Richards for supporting the visual arts in the life of the church. I would like to thank Prayer Group 12 for their unceasing prayers and for believing in me, especially Jennie Dunn for her editorial skills and her caring spirit. Sister Élise of the Community of the Holy Spirit has been a true friend in Christ. Thanks also to St. James Church and especially the Rev. Tom Faulkner for supporting my art and visual arts in the life of the Church.

My assistant and friend Michael Killfoile offered invaluable technical support especially in the making of the "Courage" series. I want to thank the many people known and unknown whose pictures appear in these pages. Last but not least, Photica processed dozens of rolls of film with great care and professionalism.

In memory of those who perished
and in thanksgiving for
the relief workers at Ground Zero
and those who supported them

Accompanying the pictorial record of the work at St. Paul's Chapel are portions of collects (topical prayers) from the Book of Common Prayer *and fragments of Scripture. These texts attempt to capture the tone and feel of the worship and service at St. Paul's Chapel. The portions of Scripture quoted are designed to comfort and encourage the hearts of all who read them. Examining the biblical verses in their broader context will provide added insight into God's providential care. Descriptions of the photographs and sources for the quotes can be found in the back of the book.*

GOD IS OUR REFUGE
AND STRENGTH,
A VERY PRESENT
HELP IN TROUBLE.
THEREFORE WE
WILL NOT FEAR
THOUGH THE EARTH
SHOULD CHANGE,
THOUGH THE
MOUNTAINS SHAKE
IN THE HEART OF
THE SEA; THOUGH
ITS WATERS ROAR
AND FOAM, THOUGH
THE MOUNTAINS
TREMBLE WITH
ITS TUMULT.

I was glad when they said unto me,
"we will go into the house of the Lord."

Defend our liberties,
and fashion into one united people
the multitudes brought hither
out of many kindreds and tongues.

my tears have been my food day and night, while
men say to me continually, "where is your god?"
why are you cast down, o my soul, and why are
you disquieted within me? hope in god;
for i shall again praise him, my help and my god.

save us from violence, discord, and confusion;
from pride and arrogance, and from every evil way.

work through
our struggle
and confusion
to accomplish
your purposes
on earth

6

LORD, keep this
nation under
your care;
and guide us
in the way of
justice and truth.

7

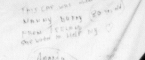

RESCUE WORKERS ONL

We are not presently open to the pub

Our ministry right now is to all of

courageous relief workers who

FOR the brave and courageous, who are patient
in suffering and faithful in adversity,
we thank you, LORD.

ʟᴏᴏᴋ ᴡɪᴛʜ ᴘɪᴛʏ upon the sorrows of thy servant
for whom our prayers are offered.

THE LORD
helps them and
delivers them;
he delivers them
from the wicked,
and saves them,
because they
take refuge
in him.

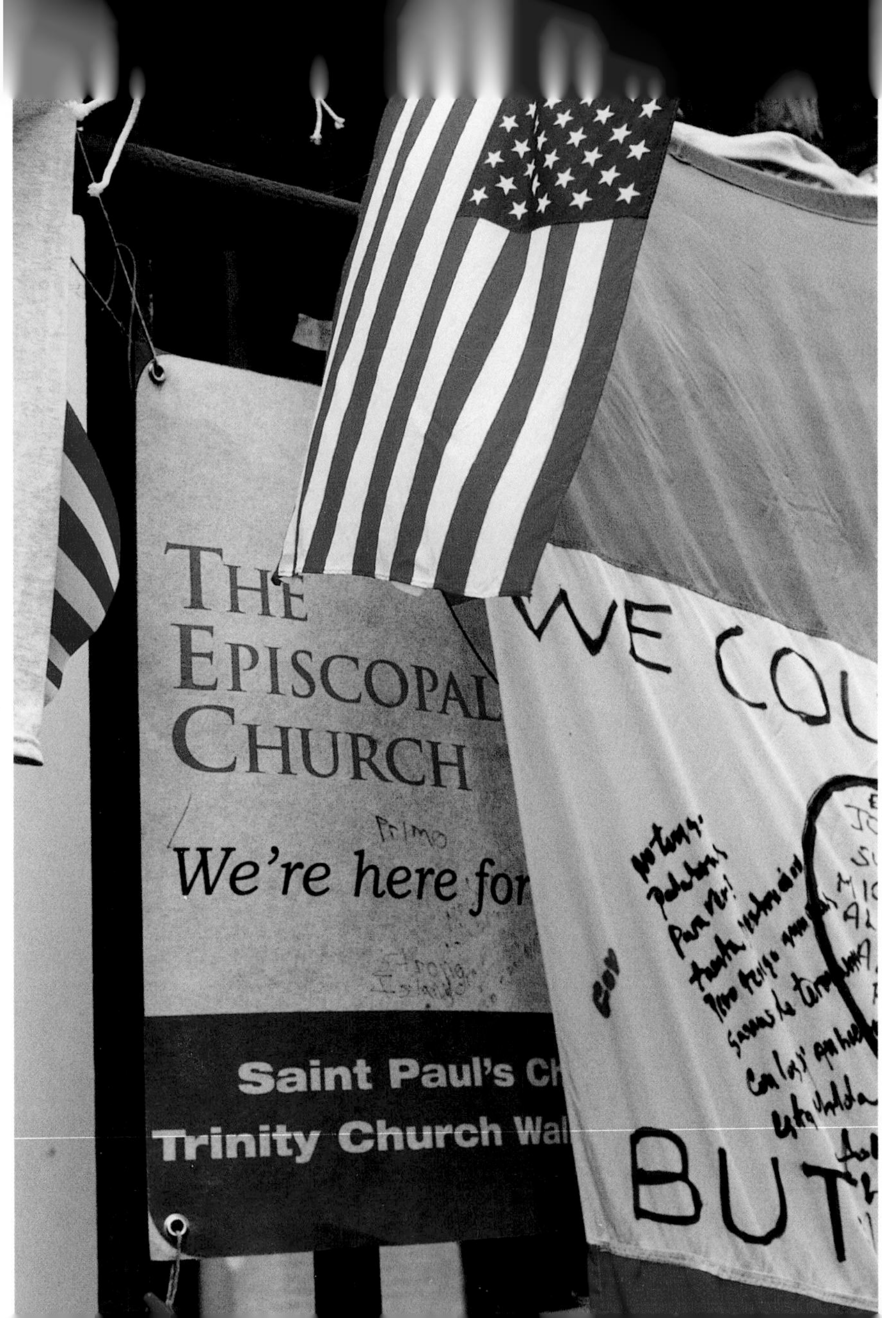

o god, whose
fatherly care
reacheth to the
uttermost parts
of the earth:
we humbly
beseech thee
graciously to
behold and bless
those whom
we love, now
absent from us.

we thank you
for the torch
of liberty
which has
been lit in
this land.

o god, the father of all, whose son commanded us
to love our enemies: lead them and us from
prejudice to truth; deliver them and us from hatred,
cruelty, and revenge; and in your good time
enable us all to stand reconciled before you;
through jesus christ our lord.

st.paul's chapel after 9/11

o god,
you have made
of one blood
all the peoples
of the earth,
and sent your
blessed son
to preach peace
to those who
are far off
and to those
who are near.

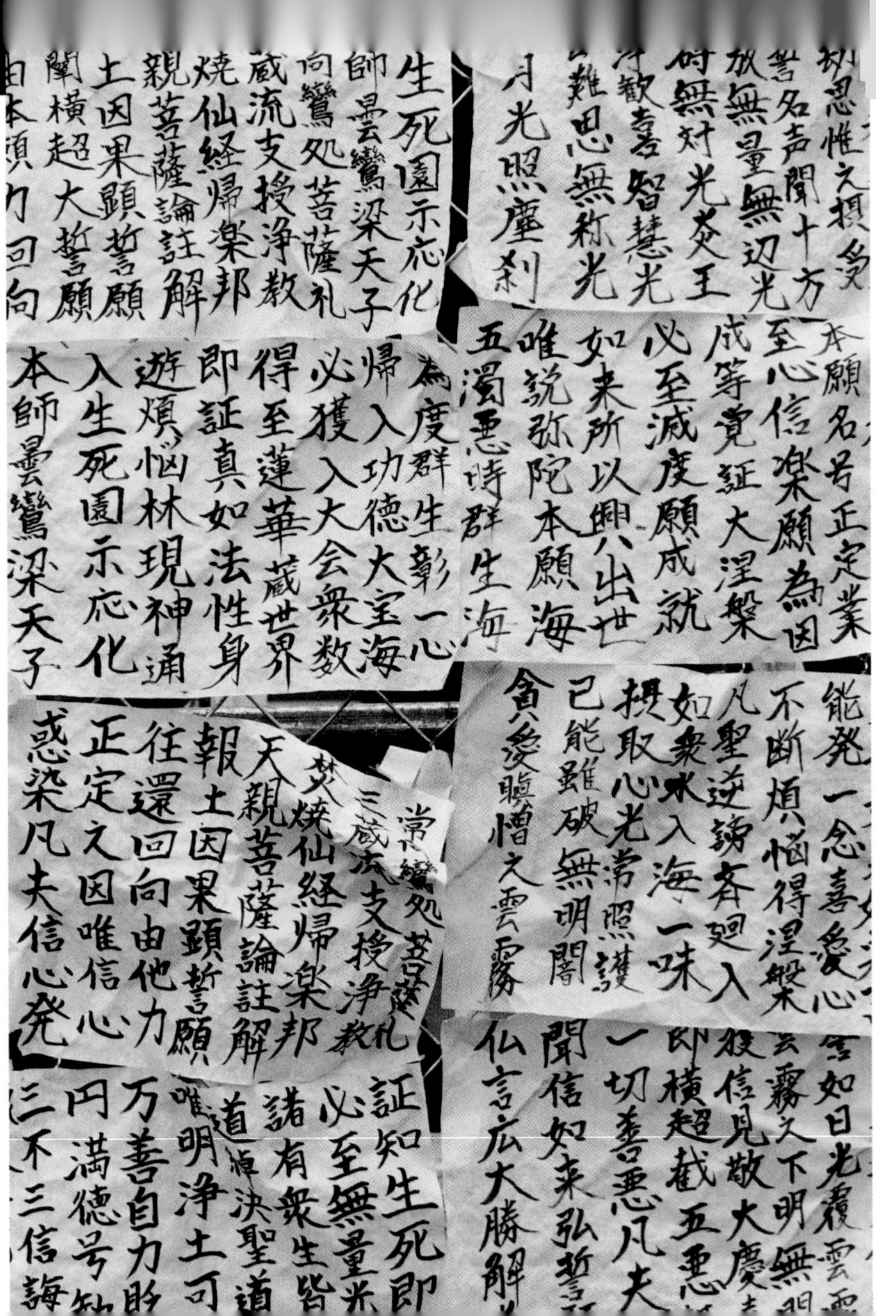

MAY the GOD of hope fill us with all joy and peace
in believing through the power of the HOly spirit.

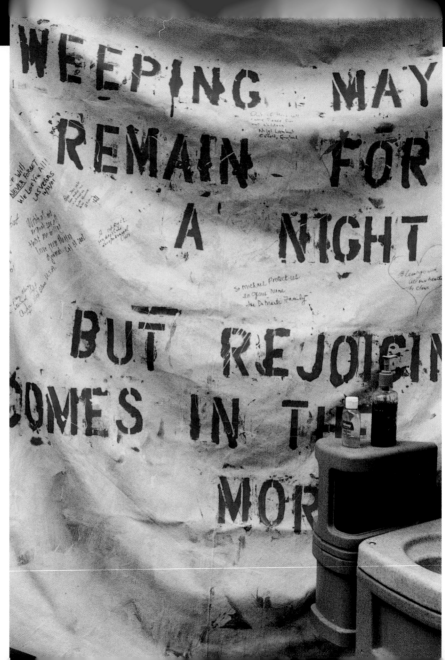

Blessed Lord,
who caused all
holy scriptures
to be written
for our learning:
Grant us so to
hear them, read,
mark, learn,
and inwardly
digest them . . .

love bears up

under anything and

everything

that comes;

It's hopes are fadeless under

all circumstances,

and it endures

everything.

1 CORINTHIANS 13:7

. . . that we
may embrace
and ever hold
fast the blessed
hope of
everlasting life,
which you have
given us in our
savior jesus
christ

17

And many of those who sleep in the dust of the earth shall awake, some to everlasting life, and some to shame and ever-lasting contempt. And those who are wise shall shine like the brightness of the firmament; and those who turn many to right-eousness, like the stars for ever and ever.

Their redeemer is strong;
the LORD of hosts is his name.

o god,
you have bound
us together in a
common life. . .

. . . Help us,
in the midst
of our struggles
for justice
and truth,
to confront
one another
without hatred
or bitterness.

21

Almighty God,
we entrust all
who are dear
to us to thy
never-failing
care and love,
for this life
and the life
to come, . . .

22

. . . knowing
that thou art
doing for them
better things
than we can
desire or pray
for; through
Jesus Christ
our Lord.

hide me
in the shadow
of thy wings,
from the wicked
who despoil me,
my deadly
enemies who
surround me.

24

For he will hide me in his shelter
in the day of trouble;
he will conceal me under
the cover of his tent,
he will set me high upon a rock.

watch over those, both night and day,
who work while others sleep . . .

. . . and grant that we may never forget that our
common life depends upon each other's toil

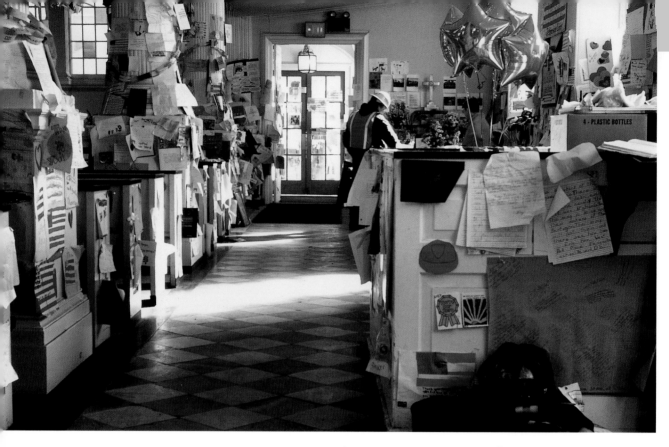

GIVE us that due sense of all thy mercies,
that our hearts may be unfeignedly thankful; . . .

. . . and that we show forth thy praise, not only with our lips, but in our lives, by giving up our selves to thy service

29

teach our people to rely on your strength
and to accept their responsibilities
to their fellow citizens.

Almighty God, our heavenly Father, guide the nations
of the world into the way of justice and truth,
and establish among them that peace which is the
fruit of righteousness, that they may become the
kingdom of our Lord and savior Jesus Christ.

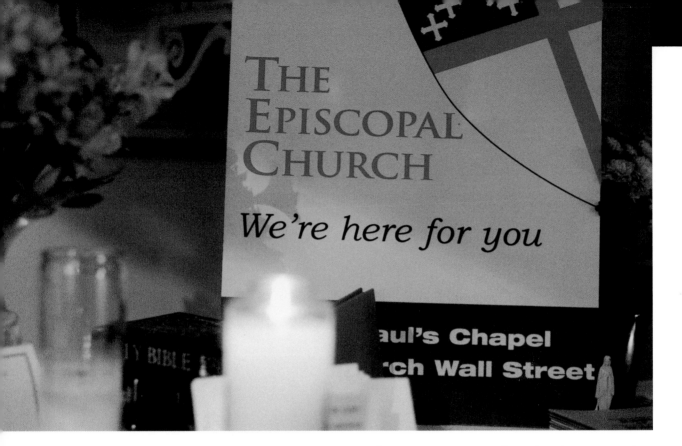

the LORD IS IN HIS holy temple;
let all the earth keep silence before him.

Lighten our darkness, we beseech thee, o Lord;
and by thy great mercy defend us from all perils and
dangers of this night; for the love of thy only son,
our savior Jesus Christ.

Defend us, thy humble servants, in all assaults of our enemies; that we, surely trusting in thy defense, may not fear the power of any adversaries.

34

LIGht dawns for the righteous,
and JOY for the upright in heart.
REJOICE in the LORD, O you righteous,
and give thanks to his holy name!

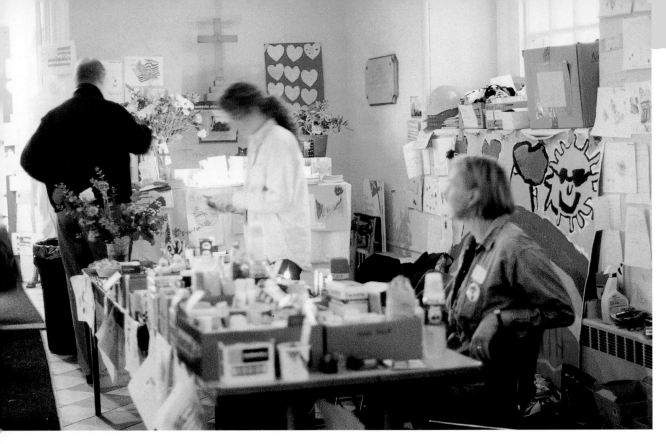

comfort and relieve them according to their
several necessities, giving them patience
under their sufferings, and a happy issue
out of all their afflictions.

we put no
obstacle in
any one's way,
so that no fault
may be found
with our
ministry, but as
servants of god
we commend
ourselves in
every way:
through great
endurance,
in afflictions,
hardships,
calamities.

They are to do good,
to be rich in good deeds,
liberal and generous

Glory to God
whose power,
working in us,
can do infinitely
more than
we can ask
or imagine:
Glory to him
from generation
to generation
in the church,
and in Christ
Jesus for ever
and ever.

so mightily spread abroad your spirit,
that all peoples may be gathered
under the banner of the PRINCE of PEACE,
as children of one FATHER.

in the time of prosperity, fill our hearts
with thankfulness, and in the day of trouble,
suffer not our trust in thee to fail

Lord, keep this nation under your care.

THE BODY OF OUR LORD JESUS CHRIST,
WHICH WAS GIVEN FOR THEE, PRESERVE THY BODY
AND SOUL UNTO EVERLASTING LIFE. TAKE AND EAT THIS
IN REMEMBRANCE THAT CHRIST DIED FOR THEE, AND FEED
ON HIM IN THY HEART BY FAITH, WITH THANKSGIVING.

grant us, in all our doubts and uncertainties,
the grace to ask what thou wouldest have us to do,
that the spirit of wisdom may save us from all false
choices, and that in thy light we may see light,
and in thy straight path may not stumble

To New York City
and all the rescuers:
Keep your spirits up...
Oklahoma loves you!!

Lift up your hearts.
we lift them up unto the Lord.

increase our reverence before the mystery of life;
and give us new insight into your purposes
for the human race, and new wisdom and
determination in making provision for its
future in accordance with your will

shine into our hearts
the brightness of your Holy spirit

NOR do men light a lamp and put it under a bushel,
but on a stand, and it gives light to all in the house.

Again Jesus spoke to them, saying, "I am the light
of the world; he who follows me will not walk
in darkness, but will have the light of life."

Almighty God, whose loving hand hath given us
all that we possess: grant us grace that we may
honor thee with our substance, and, remembering
the account which we must one day give,
may be faithful stewards of thy bounty,
through Jesus Christ our Lord.

LIGHT AT GROUND ZERO

Let the words of my mouth and the meditation
of my heart be acceptable in thy sight,
O LORD, my rock and my redeemer.

for a blessing upon all human labor,
and for the right use of the riches of creation,
that the world may be freed from poverty,
famine, and disaster, we pray to you, o lord.

keep watch,
dear Lord,
with those
who work,
or watch,
or weep
this night

endue thy
ministers with
righteousness

54

BY the might of thy spirit lift us, we pray thee,
to thy presence, where we may be still
and know that thou art GOD

o God, you made us in your own image
and redeemed us through Jesus your son:
look with compassion on the whole human family

GIVE to us, your servants, that peace
which the world cannot give.

o god, in the course of this busy life,
give us times of refreshment and peace

so enkindle fervent charity among us all, that we may
evermore be kindly affectioned one to another

Almighty God,
we commend to
your gracious care
and keeping all the
men and women of
our armed forces
at home and
abroad.

Be present, o merciful God, and protect us
through the hours of this night, so that we
who are wearied by the changes and chances
of this life may rest in your eternal changelessness;
through Jesus Christ our Lord.

O LORD, support us all the day long, until the
shadows lengthen, and the evening comes,
and the busy world is hushed, . . .

LIGHT AT GROUND ZERO

. . . and the fever of life is over, and our work
is done. Then in your mercy grant us a safe lodging,
and a holy rest, and peace at the last.

o god, who dost manifest in thy servants
the signs of thy presence: send forth upon us
the spirit of love, . . .

. . . that in companionship with one another
thine abounding grace may increase among us;
through Jesus Christ our Lord.

THE LORD
has heard my
supplication;
the LORD accepts
my prayer.

I call upon thee, for thou wilt answer me, O God;
incline thy ear to me, hear my words.

wondrously
show thy
steadfast love,
o savior of
those who seek
refuge from their
adversaries at
thy right hand.

serve the LORD with gladness!
come into his presence with singing!

o god, whom saints and angels delight to worship
in heaven: be ever present with your servants
who seek through art and music to perfect
the praises offered by your people on earth; . . .

. . . and grant
to them even
now glimpses
of your beauty,
and make them
worthy at length
to behold it
unveiled for
evermore;
through Jesus
Christ our Lord.

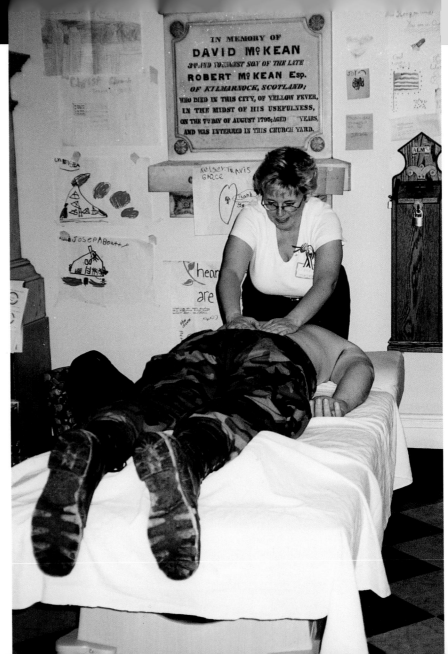

Bear one
another's
burdens, and
so fulfill the
law of christ.

72

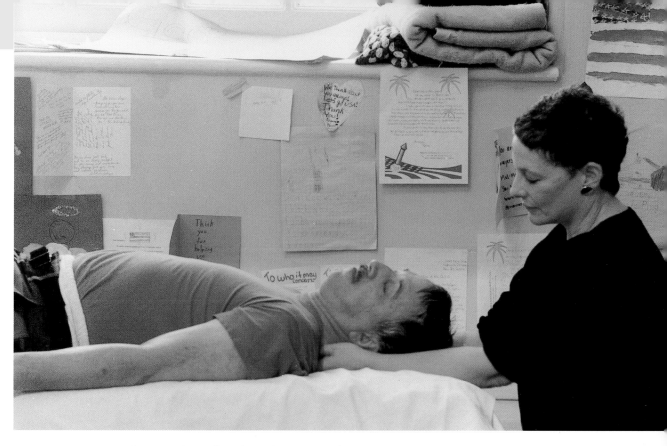

we commend to thy fatherly goodness
all those who are in any ways afflicted
or distressed, in mind, body, or estate

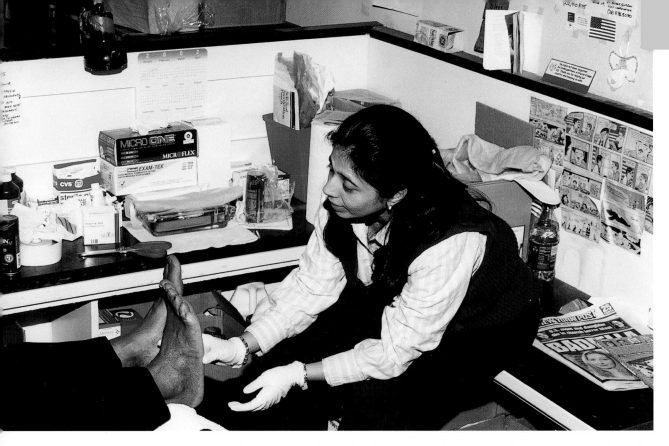

Help us to heal those who are broken in body
or spirit, and to turn their sorrow into joy.

He gives power to the faint,
and to him who has no might
he increases strength.

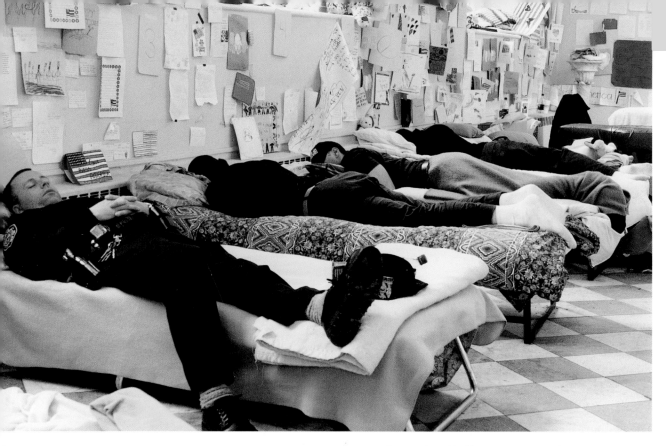

EVEN youths shall faint and be weary,
and young men shall fall exhausted

but they who
wait for the
LORD shall renew
their strength,
they shall mount
up with wings
like eagles,
they shall run
and not be
weary, they
shall walk and
not faint.

77

come to me, all who labor and are heavy laden,
and I will give you rest.

TAKE my yoke upon you, and learn from me;
for I am gentle and lowly in heart,
and you will find rest for your souls.

And the angel said to me, "write this:
blessed are those who are invited to
the marriage supper of the Lamb."

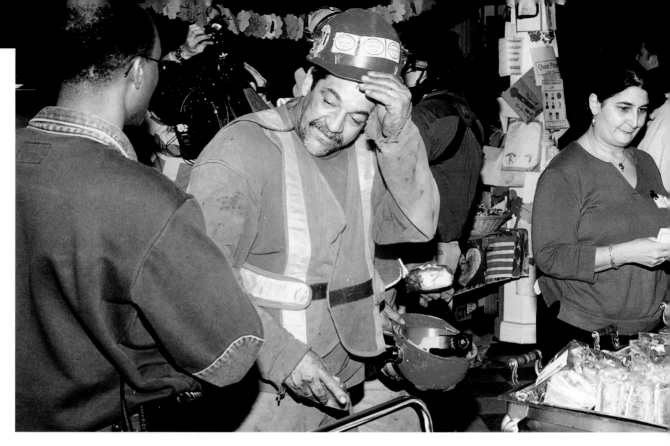

guide our feet into the way of peace;
that, having done thy will with cheerfulness
while it was day, we may, when the night cometh,
rejoice to give thee thanks

strengthen
those who
spend their lives
establishing
equal protection
of the law
and equal
opportunities
for all.

Let the favor of the Lord our God be upon us,
and establish thou the work of our hands upon us,
yea, the work of our hands establish thou it.

come, o sons, listen to me,
i will teach you the fear of the LORD.

тнιs day shall be for you a memorιal day,
and you shall keep ιt as a feast to тне Lᴏʀᴅ;
throughout your generatιons you shall observe ιt
as an ordιnance for ever.

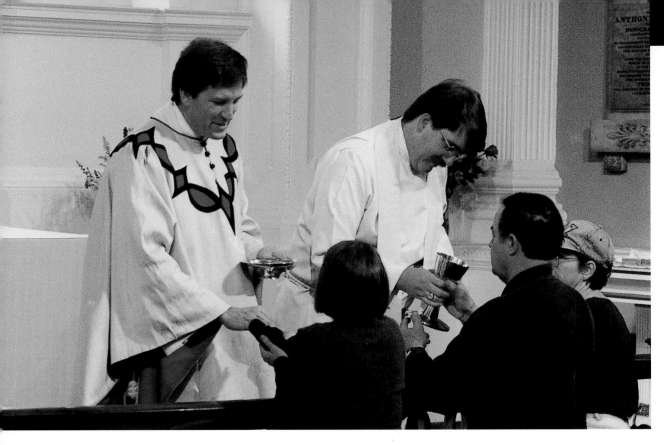

christ our passover is sacrificed for us;
therefore let us keep the feast, not with old leaven,
neither with the leaven of malice and wickedness,
but with the unleavened bread of
sincerity and truth.

THUS SAYS THE LORD:
stand by the roads, and look,
and ask for the ancient paths,
where the good way is; and walk in it,
and find rest for your souls.

"courage is fear that has said its prayers."

—Anne Lemott

LIGHT AT GROUND ZERO

Jimmy: *"I remember one little ten-year-old Spanish girl whose father died. We took her down to the site and said a prayer, then we took her by the church and gave her an angel pin and told her she would always have a guardian angel."*

Jerry: *"Most cops don't get to bond with people. Nobody calls us for happy occasions. Out of something bad something good has come. This is good. The friendships we've made. The relationships."*

—Jimmy Abbananto and Jerry Krusch, partners in the New York Police Department

"I was by the elevators, but not directly in front of them when they blew up. Those who were, were killed instantly. I was to the side. Forty percent of my body was burned. It was so random. We were instantly hit, but I was strong enough to walk down. But I'm so grateful. I didn't have the hardest part."
—Manu Dhingra,
a trader on the 84th floor
of the South Tower

"I've learned a lot about good and evil. I've learned a lot about the power of prayer. I never knew anything about Episcopalians or Presbyterians, or gays, or people with nuts and bolts through their cheeks, or those Broadway people, but now I know them all. We're not the heroes. They are the heroes. They've cried and prayed out loud for me. I never thought I'd have a family like this one."
—Joseph Bradley, a crane operator at Ground Zero

"You have men out there that are working, first on the Pile and now in the Pit, that have never worked so hard before. And then you have people inside St. Paul's and they volunteer to scrub floors, and they volunteer to haul boxes and to climb the walls and tape up letters and banners, and you have people using their gifts sacrificially to help other people."
—Katherine Avery,
St. Paul's Staff

"*For the first time in months,
I felt myself wondering if we would
ever heal from this tragedy.
Would New Yorkers be okay?
Would the workers be okay?
Would I?*"
—Sister Grace,
Sisters of St. Margaret

"If you will just try, in some small way, to open your heart to someone who needs companionship in suffering, you will discover it is an enormous gift . . . I really feel that is the deepest gift I have received from this whole experience."

—Courtney V. Cowart, Th. D., a volunteer at Ground Zero

94

*"At Ground Zero we found
something in ourselves we may
not have realized existed . . .
this reciprocity of love. It's what
I think we can draw from 9/11."*

—Martin Cowart,
food captain at St. Paul's

95

"The destruction was overwhelming but I've never seen such courage, love and strength."

—Rebecca Pruthi, podiatrist, with her partner Debra Manheim

The crisis called for
people with many different
job descriptions. State Trooper
Bob Allen from Oxford, New York.

Firefighters paid a high price.
Those who survived carried on
their work faithfully, heeding
neither fatigue nor despair.

The rescue workers
labored in unimaginable
conditions—sixteen hours or more,
day after day, with no days off.

Foreword *"When we either individually or collectively face death, there is a space opened up in which we can appreciate all the more the precious gift of life and to affirm that our connectedness is far greater than our divisions. . . The Creator of the Universe loves us so much that nothing—absolutely nothing—will separate us from our God's love for us. Not height, nor depth, nor angels, nor principalities, things present, nor things to come, nor terrorists. . . "*
—The Rev. Lyndon F. Harris, Associate for Ministries at St. Paul's Chapel, wearing a chasuble stitched with patches of emergency crews.

1. The 18th century steeple of St. Paul's Chapel overlooks the World Trade Center site several months into the recovery and cleanup operation. The chapel and churchyard were virtually unharmed when the colossal towers collapsed a few hundred feet away.
Psalm 46:1–3

2. The day after the disaster, St. Paul's was converted into a relief center for workers at Ground Zero. The relief project continued 24 hours a day for nearly nine months.
Psalm 122:1

3. When the west side of Broadway was finally opened to the public, thousands came to pay their respects and add their written prayers and sentiments to the posters and banners festooning the chapel's iron fence. The chapel itself remained closed to the public for many more months.
Prayer for our Country

4. The fence around St. Paul's became a spontaneous memorial to those who perished in the WTC attack and a bulletin board carrying notes of encouragement and appreciation to those who carried on the arduous work in the following months.
Psalm 42:3, 5–6A

5. While the chapel was closed to the public, round-the-clock volunteer gate keepers carried on an important ministry to all those who entered or passed by.
Prayer for our Country

6. The red New York City Fire Department cross was placed on the fence very early on. Colored ribbons, caps, letters and notes were added daily.
Prayer for the Human Family

7. Flags, handmade banners, plaques, buttons, even tee shirts were hung on the fence wherever there was an empty space.
Morning and Evening Prayer

8. Visitors to St. Paul's wore many different hats but had one heart.
Litany of Thanksgiving

9. Chaplain Bob from Illinois, a regular volunteer, prayed with hundreds of people in the chapel and on the street. A nun made the trip to St. Paul's specifically to be a "praying presence."
For a person in trouble or bereavement

10. Church and state mingle in shameless solidarity.
Psalm 37:40

11. Mini-shrines abounded. Here Jesus coexists peacefully with a plastic angel, an American flag, a Hebrew greeting card and a bouquet of fresh flowers.
Prayer for the Absent

12. Thousands of candles burned day and night, inside and outside.
Thanksgiving for the Nation

13. The disaster prompted an abundance of creative output: here, an American flag made from prints of children's hands.
Prayer for our enemies

14. Messages of love and support arrived in many languages.
Prayer for Mission

15-18. These banners, and the "Courage" banner (#88) were made by Jessica Stammen and students from The Cooper Union.
Romans 15:13
Proper 28
Daniel 12:2–3

19. Writings and artwork by children were prominent among the thousands of messages sent to the chapel.
Jeremiah 50:34A

20-23. Many shared their sorrow and their faith by signing one of the canvases strung along Broadway.
Prayer in Times of Conflict
Prayer for those we Love

24. The present collection represents one of very few exceptions to the rule prohibiting photos and videos. It was a challenge trying to record the event without violating the privacy of those using the chapel.
Psalm 17:8B–9

25. The view of Broadway from the front door. For months, at every hour of the day and night, spectators patiently stood in line on the other side of Broadway to get a view of Ground Zero from Fulton Street or John Street.
Psalm 27:5

26. It was sometimes awkward photographing people having their dinner. These police officers were very obliging.
Compline

27. The Classic Revival porch with its brown fluted columns hosted three meals a day until the onset of cold weather at the end of November forced the food service inside the chapel. In the course of eight months some 5,000 volunteers served half a million meals.

compline

28-29. Children's cards and letters papered the walls, covered the pews, and climbed up columns and staircases. There were so many letters that the church staff would spread unopened letters in the pews for visitors to open and read.

The General Thanksgiving

30. Gourmet meals arrived piping hot in special steel cabinets from the Waldorf Astoria and fine restaurants throughout the city. All the food and its preparation and delivery were donated, along with mountains of supplies ranging from work boots to eye drops.

Prayer For Sound Government

31. The balcony railings provided an ideal display space for a fraction of the hundreds of banners from around the world. The banners were changed frequently so that as many as possible could be displayed. Every pew in the north gallery was crammed with supplies, making the chapel a hardware store, a pharmacy, and a clothing store.

Prayer For Peace Among the Nations

32. A small altar just inside the door became a spontaneous shrine with flowers and candles.

Habakkuk 2:20

33. The shrine changed daily. There were always new cards, new pictures, and fresh flowers.

collect for Aid against Perils

34. Photographs of the lost and missing were interspersed with cards, religious objects and candles. It was many months before some of the bereaved families would be willing to admit that their loved one, whose body was never recovered or identified, had not survived.

A Collect for Peace

35. Katherine Avery coordinated the relief operation for nearly nine months. Her skillful organizing and cheerful presence were the heartbeat of the entire project. Her cell phone was permanently attached to her ear. There were thousands of calls from churches, synagogues, offices and private individuals eager to serve. Not everybody could be accommodated. Service was a privilege.

Psalm 97:11–12

36. As you came in from Broadway you encountered the tables offering the most frequently requested items. Boot inserts were particularly popular (boot soles were sometimes burned through from prolonged contact with red hot beams). Aspirin and eye drops were

much in demand. For weeks the entire New York area, but especially the vicinity of Ground Zero, was covered with smoke from fires deep in the rubble that would not be extinguished.
Prayer For All sorts and Conditions of Men

37. Diane, another coordinator of volunteers.
2 Corinthians 6:3–4

38. In April the Cooper Union art students created a stirring new banner painted with the help of workers from the site.
1 Timothy 6:18

39. Incongruous juxtapositions were everywhere. Here a demure plaque honoring a distinguished vestryman shares its space with children's cards and cartons of cheese and crackers.
Ephesians 3:20,21

40. View of the west (back) wall of the chapel. The door leads to the churchyard facing Ground Zero, but volunteers were firmly instructed not to approach the site from any direction. The banner directly above the aisle is from Duesseldorf, Germany.
Prayer for Peace

41. Box pews may not seem like the ideal place to eat or sleep, but they were very welcome to tired and hungry workers. Quiet conversation was never discouraged. Some prayed, some just sat with their private reflections. The dozen or so cots along the north wall were a coveted luxury.
Prayer for Our Country

42. Next to the pulpit an American flag composed of photos of the victims screened massage tables in constant use. A nearby column was entirely wrapped in a dramatic banner, "Oklahoma Sends Love."
Morning and Evening Prayer

43-44. Almost the only place in the chapel that did not say "9/11" was the white-and-gold pulpit and altar with the expanse of east-facing windows, an ever-changing light show.
Holy Eucharist
Prayer for Guidance

45. Oklahoma was understandably well represented, sharing its empathy from the 1995 Oklahoma City bombing.
Holy Eucharist

46. Flag of remembrance composed of photos of the missing.
Prayer for the Future of the Human Race

47-49. Candles of St. Paul's Chapel. Candles burned 24 hours a day, seven days a week, reminding us of those who died and of the presence of the Holy Spirit.
Order for Evening
Matthew 5:15
John 8:12

50. Cough drops were a necessity for those working long hours in the acrid heat of the pit.
Prayer for the Right Use of God's Gifts

51. More than 300 canvases hung on the Broadway fence were filled with inscriptions by passersby. When a canvas was full it would be replaced by a clean one.
Psalm 19:14

52. The homely paraphernalia of grownups and children.
Prayers of the People

53-63. Firefighters, firemen's chaplains, FDNY paramedics, sanitation workers, construction workers, national guard, police officers, crane operators, rescue workers and demolition experts came from Ground Zero. They were there getting their brothers and sisters out. They were our heroes. They came to St. Paul's to rest, to eat, to talk, to let go. Nobody asked questions. We didn't know who identified body parts and who worked with twisted girders and crumbled concrete. We chatted, cried, joked, prayed. The mood was strangely upbeat but we could see the exhaustion, and sometimes the despair. We also saw the courage, the selfless service, and the determination to carry on.
Evening Prayer
Morning and Evening Prayer
Prayer for Quiet Confidence
Prayer for the Human Family

collect for Peace
Prayer for the Good Use of Leisure
Prayers for Families
Prayer for those in the Armed Forces
compline
Prayer in the Evening

64. Firefighters display a cross made from links found at Ground Zero.
Evening Prayer

65. Goodbyes on June 2 were hard, emotional, bittersweet.
Evening Prayer

66-68. Sometimes it's hard to pray outside. In church, praying is okay, and many availed themselves of the opportunity.
Psalm 6:9
Psalm 17:6
Psalm 17:7

69-71. Violinists, pianists, guitar players, flutists and orchestras played Bach, Chopin and Mozart. As the sounds filled the chapel everybody realized how badly it was needed, how badly beauty was needed.
Psalm 100:2
Prayer for Church Musicians and Artists

72-73. It was touching and intimate to see men's exhausted bodies being massaged by the tender loving hands of professional masseuses.
Galatians 6:2
Prayer for All Sorts and Conditions of Men

74. George Washington's box pew became a podiatrist's office. Blistered feet got a lot of attention.
Prayer for the Poor and the Neglected

75-79. There were always stocks of blankets for those who wanted to sleep or just rest. Tired workers slept in pews and in the cots downstairs and in the west balcony. One time during Eucharist the snoring was so loud that we barely heard the words of the liturgy. Nobody raised an eyebrow.
Isaiah 40:29–31
Matthew 11:28–29

80-82. When the weather turned cold the food service moved from the Broadway porch to the back of the chapel. There were scrambled eggs with bacon in the morning, Zabar sandwiches and hot soup for lunch, and delicious hot dinners. There was no lack of snack foods: candy, granola bars, power bars, tea and coffee, mountains of canned soda, and toward the end . . . cappuccino. Everybody ate in the pews.
Revelation 19:9
Collect for the Renewal of Life
Prayer for the Oppressed

83. This enormous banner from the Spartanburg, South Carolina Elementary School arrived on Valentine's Day.
Psalm 90:17

84-86. The Rev. Lyndon F. Harris, Associate for Ministries at St. Paul's Chapel, was a loving presence who always had time to talk, to pray, to give encouraging words, a smile, a hug to the hundreds of people visiting the chapel: workers, volunteers, health professionals, the bereaved, TV crews, journalists, government officials and visitors from around the world. Through it all he faithfully carried out his duties as a priest.
Psalm 34:11
Exodus 12:14
1 Corinthians 5:7–8

87. Thousands stood in the cold to view Ground Zero from the viewing platform on Fulton Street, next to the St. Paul's cemetery.
Jeremiah 6:16

88. This banner by Jessica Stammen (designed for collaborative participation by the public) became the backdrop for the series "Courage": portraits of police, firefighters, construction workers, crane operators, national guard and St. Paul's staff.

Glory to God, whose power, working in us, can do infinitely more than we can ask or imagine: Glory to him from generation to generation in the Church, and in Christ Jesus for ever and ever. Amen.

Krystyna Sanderson, a fine art and commercial photographer, has been widely exhibited and her work is in public and private collections in the U.S. and Europe. Her photographic series "Masks" was published in book form by Texas Tech Press. She is a contributing author of a chapter on "Light" in the book *It Was Good: Making Art to the Glory of God,* published by Square Halo Books in 2000.

For close to eight months Krystyna photographed the relief project at St. Paul's Chapel, one block from Ground Zero, and produced over 2,500 images. Photographs from the series were presented at Harvard Medical School, Virginia Theological Seminary and General Theological Seminary; have appeared in *The Episcopal New Yorker, Episcopal Life, Spirituality and Health* and *Trinity News;* and can be viewed at www.ecva.org ("Since September 11..."), www.saintpaulschapel.org and www.national-geographic.com ("Sanctuary at Ground Zero"). Krystyna holds an M.F.A. in painting and photography from Texas Tech University.

She taught photography at The New School and at St. John's University and was a staff photographer for the New York City Police

ANDREW J.N.GARY

Department. She is a member of the board of directors of ECVA (The Episcopal Church and Visual Arts). Krystyna and her husband Colin worship at Grace Episcopal Church in New York.

FAITH

"SQUARE HALO IS QUICKLY BECOMING A LEADER IN THE REALM OF CHRISTIANITY AND THE ARTS"

+ART

It Was Good: Making Art to the Glory of God is a collection of thirteen essays—including one by Krystyna Sanderson—covering a wide range of topics focussed on the practice of making art from a Christian worldview. "We recommend *It Was Good: Making Art to the Glory of God* to you. It will help you think Christianly about art, stimulate you to be creative for God's glory, introduce you to some artists who are seeking to glorify God in their work, and … cause you to stop and worship the One whose glory is beautiful beyond all imagining." —CRITIQUE

ISBN# 0-9658798-2-8

"Objects of Grace: Conversations on Creativity and Faith is a colorful and concise collection of interviews and art from some of America's most intriguing Christian artists … Sandra Bowden, Dan Callis, Mary McCleary, John Silvis, Edward Knippers, Erica Downer, Albert Pedulla, Tim Rollins, Joel Sheesley, and Makoto Fujimura. This group gives a vivid account of what it means for God's grace to be incarnated into the visual arts in our postmodern world … The sheer beauty of the design and production values of this book is itself a major achievement, one that gives hope both for the church and the larger culture." —*IMAGE: A JOURNAL OF THE ARTS & RELIGION

ISBN# 0-9658798-3-6

www.SquareHaloBooks.com